50 FAMOUS PEOPLE IN MODERN HISTORY FOR KIDS

BABY PROFESSOR
EDUCATION KIDS

Speedy Publishing LLC
40 E. Main St. #1156
Newark, DE 19711
www.speedypublishing.com

Copyright 2016

All Rights reserved. No part of this book may be reproduced or used in any way or form or by any means whether electronic or mechanical, this means that you cannot record or photocopy any material ideas or tips that are provided in this book

50 FAMOUS PEOPLE IN MODERN HISTORY FOR KIDS

1. **Abraham Lincoln (1809 – 1865)** He was the 16th US President. He was best known for leading the country during the Civil War. He was also called Honest Abe.

2. **Adolf Hitler (1889 – 1945)** He was the leader of Nazi Germany, which ran from 1933 to 1945. He believed that Germans were born to rule over others. Hitler's offensives sparked the World War II.

3. **Albert Einstein (1879 – 1955)** He was a German scientist and was considered a brilliant physicist. He authored the theory of relativity that led to breakthroughs in science and research, such as the atomic energy.

ALBERT EINSTEIN

ADOLF HITLER

AMELIA EARHART

50 FAMOUS PEOPLE IN MODERN HISTORY FOR KIDS

4. **Amelia Earhart (1897 – 1937)** She was an American aviation pioneer. Earhart was the first female aviator to fly solo across the Atlantic Ocean. Her disappearance became the most intriguing mystery in the 20th century.

5. **Barack Obama (1961 –)** He was the 44th US President. He was elected twice and served two terms, from 2008 to 2016. He was the first African-American to win the presidency.

6. **Bill Gates (1955 –)** He was a computer programmer before He became a successful businessman. In 1975, Bill founded Microsoft.

50 FAMOUS PEOPLE IN MODERN HISTORY FOR KIDS

7. **Charlie Chaplin (1889 – 1977)** – He was one of the most famous characters seen in movies. He was famous for his ridiculous mustache, derby hat and cane.

8. **Charles Darwin (1809 – 1882)** He was a British scientist. Charles Darwin authored of Theory of Evolution. He revolutionized the study of living things.

9. **Christopher Columbus (1451 – 1506)** He was an Italian explorer who first discovered America. His arrival paved the way for Western Civilization in America.

CHARLES DARWIN

CHRISTOPHER COLUMBUS

CHARLIE CHAPLIN

DALAI LAMA

50 FAMOUS PEOPLE IN MODERN HISTORY FOR KIDS

10. Coco Chanel (1883 – 1971) She was a French fashion designer who introduced the world of high-fashion in Paris. She inspired women to wear elegant and casual designs.

11. Dalai Lama (1938 –) He is a spiritual and political leader of the Tibetans. He is the head of a religious order called Dge-lugs-pa (or Yellow Hat).

12. David Beckham (1975 –) He is an English footballer. He popularized the "Bend it like Beckham" because his powerfulkicks would cause the ball to bend around players. He is very good in free kicks and crosses.

50 FAMOUS PEOPLE IN MODERN HISTORY FOR KIDS

13. **Donald Trump (1946 –)** He is a famous businessman and billionaire, who won the 2016 US Presidential Election against Hillary Clinton. He made history by being the first President with no previous political or military experience.

14. **Elvis Presley (1935 – 1977)** He was an American musician known as the King of Rock and Roll.

15. **George Washington (1732 – 1799)** –He was the first President of the United States. He was the Leader of the U.S. Forces during the American Revolution.

GEORGE WASHINGTON AND HIS GENERALS

ELVIS PRESLEY

50 FAMOUS PEOPLE IN MODERN HISTORY FOR KIDS

16. Isaac Newton (1642 – 1727) – He was a British mathematician and scientist. He was known as the main figure of the scientific revolution in the 17th century. He created calculus and the three laws of motion.

17. Pope Francis (1936 –) He is the first pope from the Americas. He is the 266th Bishop of Rome and the head of the Roman Catholic Church.

18. J.K.Rowling (1965 –) She is the author of the world famous Harry Potter books and movies. She used magic and witchcraft to capture the imagination of her readers. The Harry Potter books are the best-selling books in today's era.

50 FAMOUS PEOPLE IN MODERN HISTORY FOR KIDS

19. Kim Jong Un – He is the leader of North Korea. He is the successor of Kim Jong Il, his Father. He represents the third generation of the Kim dynasty.

20. Pope John Paul II (1920 – 2005) He was a Polish Pope. He was the 264th Bishop of Rome. He was the longest reigning Pope in the history of the Roman Catholic Church.

21. John F. Kennedy (1917 – 1963) He was the 35th US President, who served from 1961 to 1963. He was the youngest elected president of the United States. He died by assassination.

ISAAC NEWTON

50 FAMOUS PEOPLE IN MODERN HISTORY FOR KIDS

22. **John Lennon (1940 – 1980)** He was a British musician and a member of the band The Beatles. The Beatles' music and culture made a strong impact in the 1960's.

23. **Leonardo da Vinci (1452 – 1519)** He was a famous Italian painter, scientist and polymath. His was famous for masterpieces like Mona Lisa and The Last Supper.

24. **Ludwig Beethoven (1770 – 1827)** He was a famous German composer. He bridged the gap between the 18th-century classical period and the new beginnings of Romanticism. His most influential pieces were symphonies and instrumental work.

50 FAMOUS PEOPLE IN MODERN HISTORY FOR KIDS

25. **Madonna (1958 –)** She is an American musician, actress and author. She became a worldwide pop sensation in the 1980's.

26. **Mahatma Gandhi (1869 – 1948)** He was a National Hero. He was the leader of the Indian Independence Movement. He ended the British rule over Native India without force and bloodshed.

27. **Marilyn Monroe (1926 – 1962)** She was an American actress, singer and model. She was known for her glamour, sex appeal and innocence.

JOHN F. KENNEDY

LEONARDO DA VINCI

MAHATMA GANDHI

50 FAMOUS PEOPLE IN MODERN HISTORY FOR KIDS

28. **Mark Zuckerberg** – He is an American computer programmer. He is the founder of the famous social networking website Facebook.

29. **Martin Luther King (1929 – 1968)** He was an American civil rights campaigner. He was one of the outstanding black leaders in the United States. He was a Nobel Prize Winner for nonviolent resistance to oppression.

30. **Michael Jackson (1958 – 2009)** He was an American musician. He was known as the King of Pop. He was famous for his dance moves in songs like Thriller and Beat it.

50 FAMOUS PEOPLE IN MODERN HISTORY FOR KIDS

31. **Michael Jordan (1963 –)** He is an American Basketball star, who is one of the greatest all-around players in the history of basketball. He was famous for his slam dunk and the logo Air Jordan.

32. **Mother Teresa (1910 – 1997)** She was a Macedonian Catholic missionary and was one of the most highly respected women in the world. She won a Nobel Prize for her humanitarian deeds.

33. **Muhammad Ali (1942 – 2016)** He was a famous American Boxer, who was also a civil rights campaigner. He was famous for his motto "I am the greatest!"

MAHATMA GANDHI STATUE

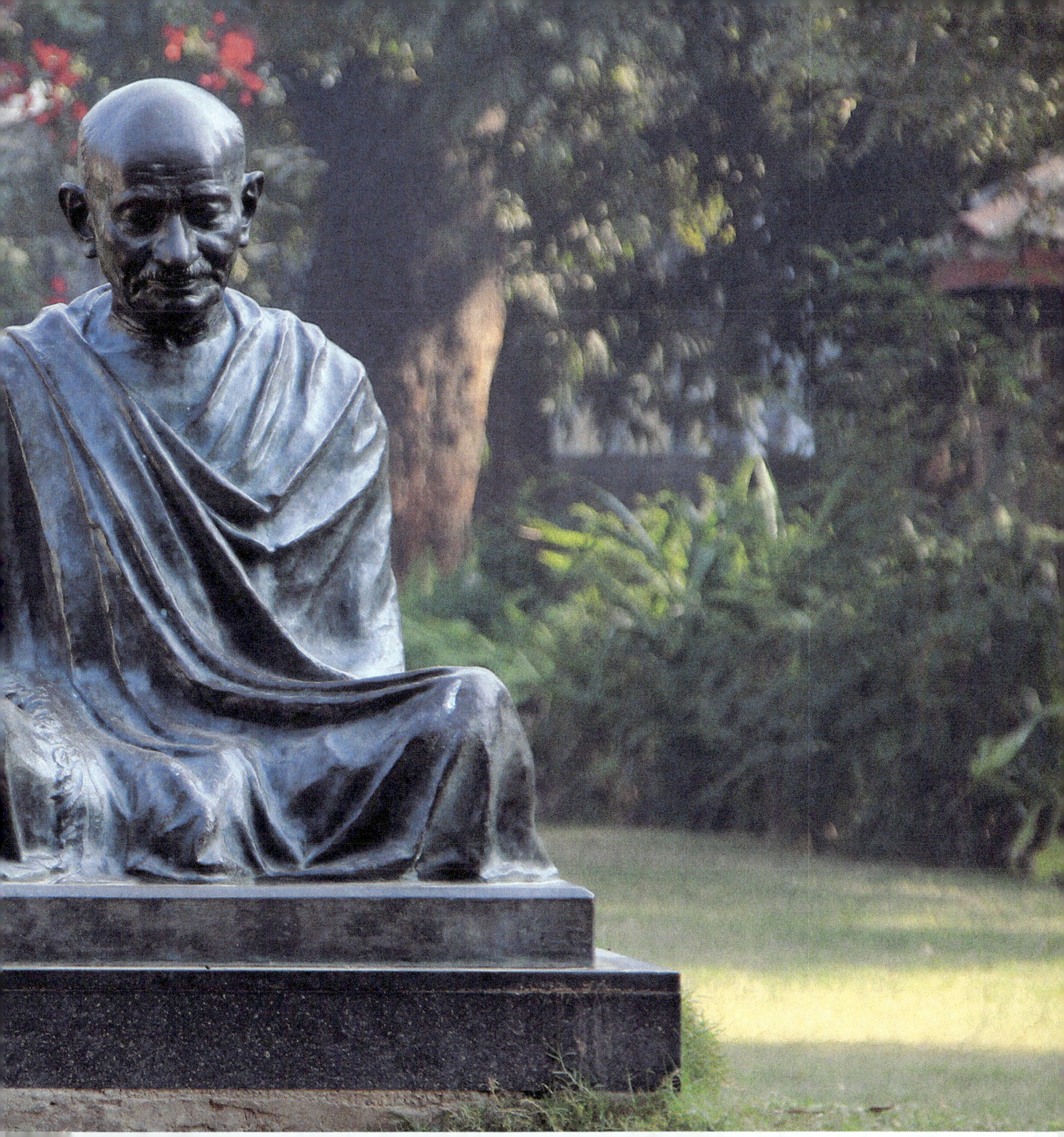

50 FAMOUS PEOPLE IN MODERN HISTORY FOR KIDS

34. **Nelson Mandela (1918 – 2013)** He was the famous South African President who was also a political prisoner for 27 years. He was an South African activist and fought for peace and equal human rights.

35. **Neil Armstrong (1930 – 2012)** He was an American Astronaut. He was the first person to set foot on the Moon. He said the famous quote "That's one small step for [a] man, one giant leap for mankind."

36. **Osama Bin Laden** – He founded and financed a terrorist group known as al-Quaeda. He was the leader of an Islamic extremist movement that led to the terrorist attack in the United States on Sept. 11, 2001.

MARILYN MONROE

MICHAEL JACKSON

MOTHER TERESA

50 FAMOUS PEOPLE IN MODERN HISTORY FOR KIDS

37. **Oprah Winfrey (1954 –)** She is a famous American celebrity. She is also considered as one of the most successful women in entertainment industry.

38. **Pablo Picasso (1881 – 1973)** He was a famous Spanish modern artist. His art led to different movements in the 20th century. He also became a sculptor, engraver, and ceramist.

39. **Pelé (1940 –)** He is a Brazilian footballer. He is a football superstar in the 20th century. He is also the highest-paid athlete when he joined the North American Team.

NELSON MANDELA

NEIL ARMSTRONG

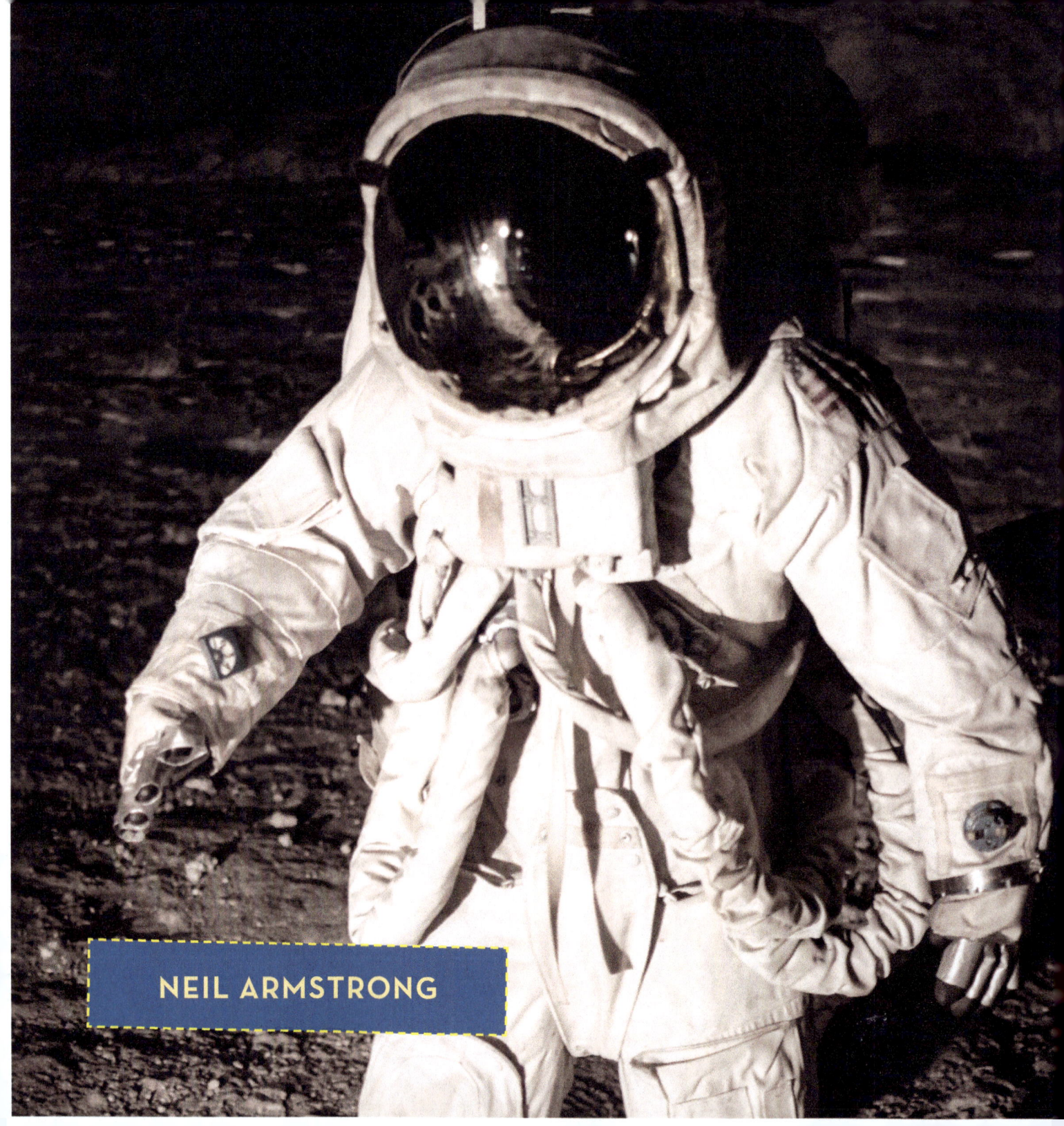

300 F

21e ANNIVERSAIRE LADY DIANA, 1er JUILLET 1982
1980 LADY DIANA NURSE A LONDRES

POSTE AERIENNE

REPUBLIQUE DU TCHAD

IMPRESSOR S.A. (SWITZERLAND)

PRINCESS DIANA

VINCENT VAN GOGH

50 FAMOUS PEOPLE IN MODERN HISTORY FOR KIDS

40. **Princess Diana (1961- 1997)** She was the famous Princess of Wales. She was the first wife of Charles, Prince of Wales. She became an international obsession because of her charm and good deeds.

41. **Tiger Woods (1975)** He is a famous American golfer. He achieved worldwide fame by winning many major golf championship titles.

42. **Thomas Edison (1847 – 1931)** He was an American inventor. He influenced life around the world by inventing many devices like the phonograph, motion camera and the famous long-lasting light bulb.

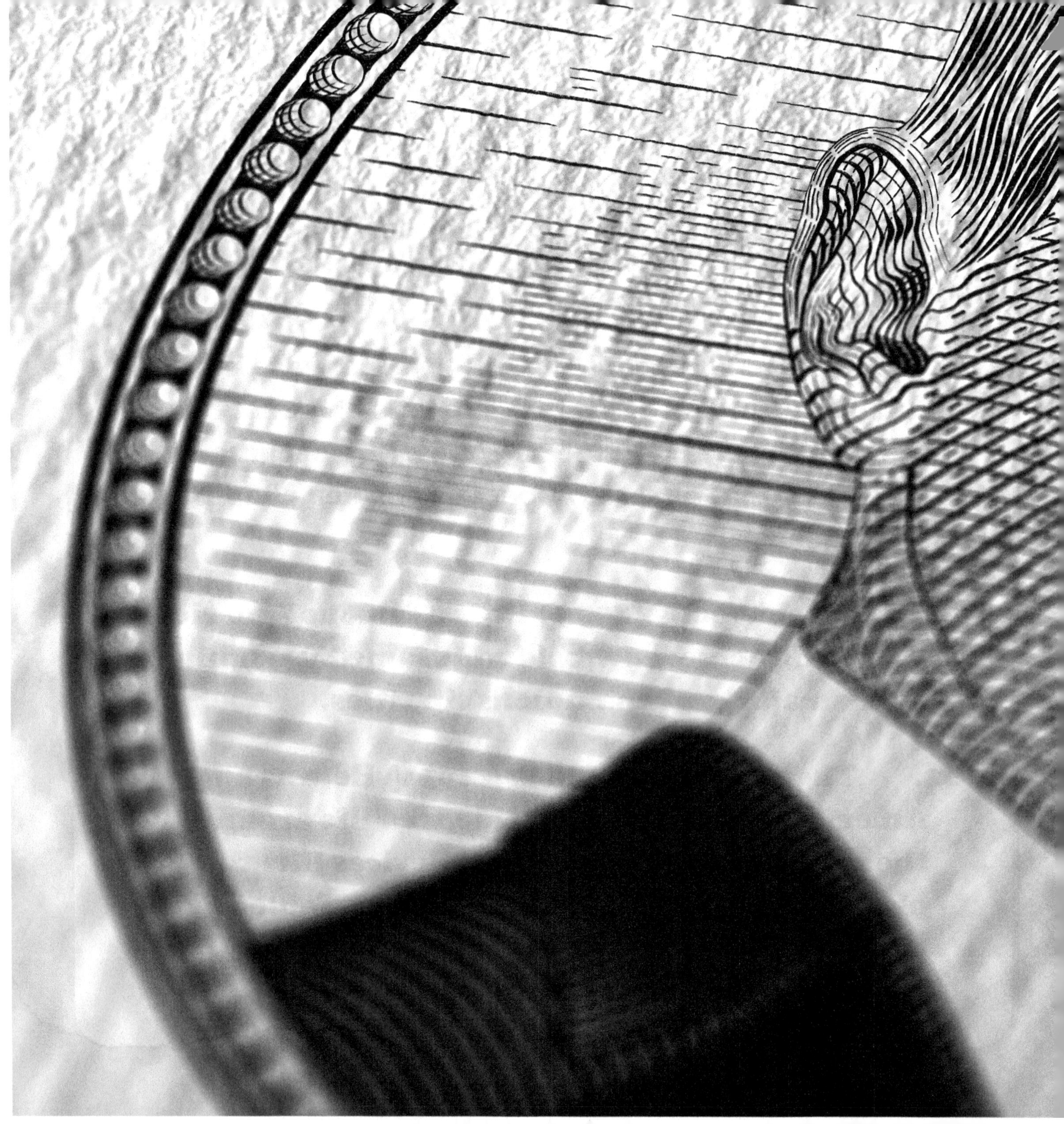

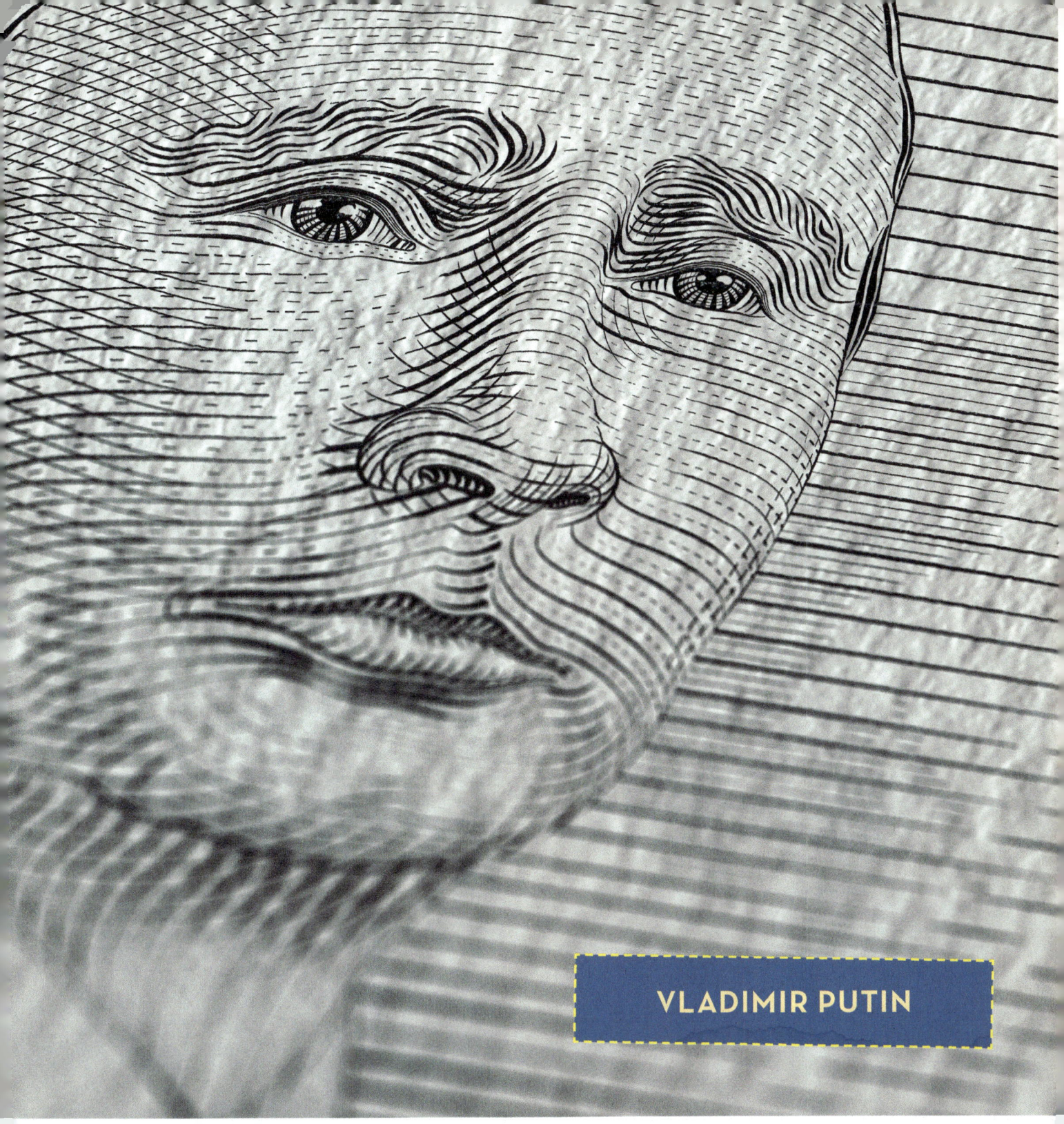

VLADIMIR PUTIN

THOMAS EDISON

50 FAMOUS PEOPLE IN MODERN HISTORY FOR KIDS

43. **Steve Jobs (1955 – 2012)** He was an American businessman. He was the famous co-founder of Apple computers.

44. **Usain Bolt (1986 –)** He is a Jamaican athlete and Olympian. He was nicknamed as the "lightning bolt". He won many gold medals in Olypmic races and was considered as the greatest sprinter of all time.

45. **Vincent Van Gogh (1853 – 1890)** He was one of the greatest Dutch artists after Rembrandt. He had a powerful influence on expressionism in modern life. His greatest work was the famous Starry Night.

WINSTON CHURCHILL

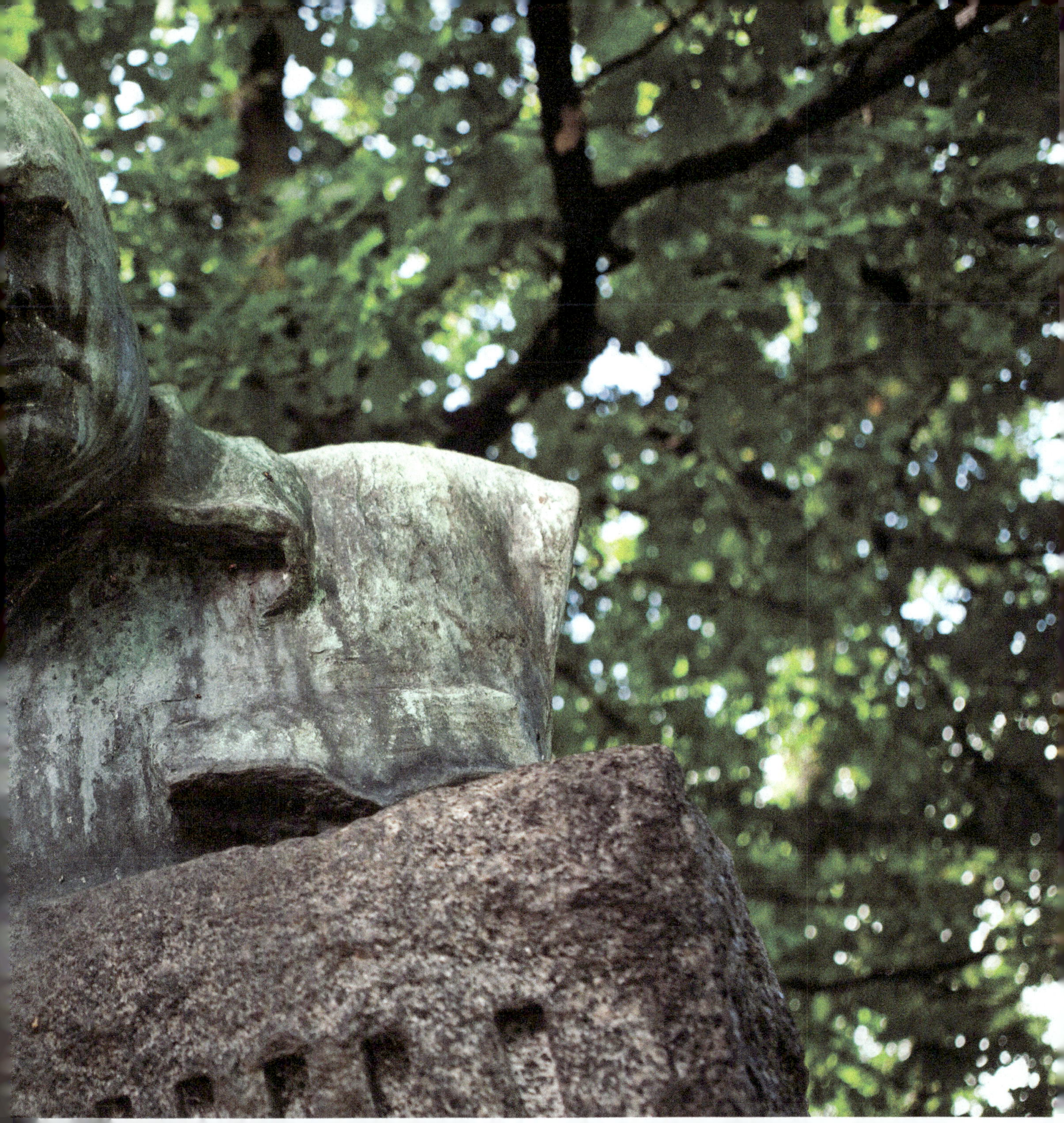

50 FAMOUS PEOPLE IN MODERN HISTORY FOR KIDS

46. **Vladimir Putin – (1952)** He is the present Russian President. He was the Prime Minister of Russia from 1999 to 2000. He was also the President from 2000 to 2008.

47. **Walt Disney (1901 – 1966)** He was an American film producer, cartoonist and master of motion picture animation. He created Mickey Mouse.

48. **William Shakespeare (1564- 1616)** He was an English poet and playwright. His works are read and played in theater all around the world until today. His works have been translated in almost all languages and have inspired thousands of adaptations like movies and stage plays.

50 FAMOUS PEOPLE IN MODERN HISTORY FOR KIDS

49. **Winston Churchill (1874 – 1965)** He was a British Prime Minister during World War II. He was one of the greatest leaders that stood against Hitler.

50. **Wright Brothers Orville (1871 – 1948) and Wilbur (1867 – 1912)** They were the famous American brother-inventors that created and flew the first airplane. Their invention was a milestone for modern transportation. They were the pioneers in the area of flight.

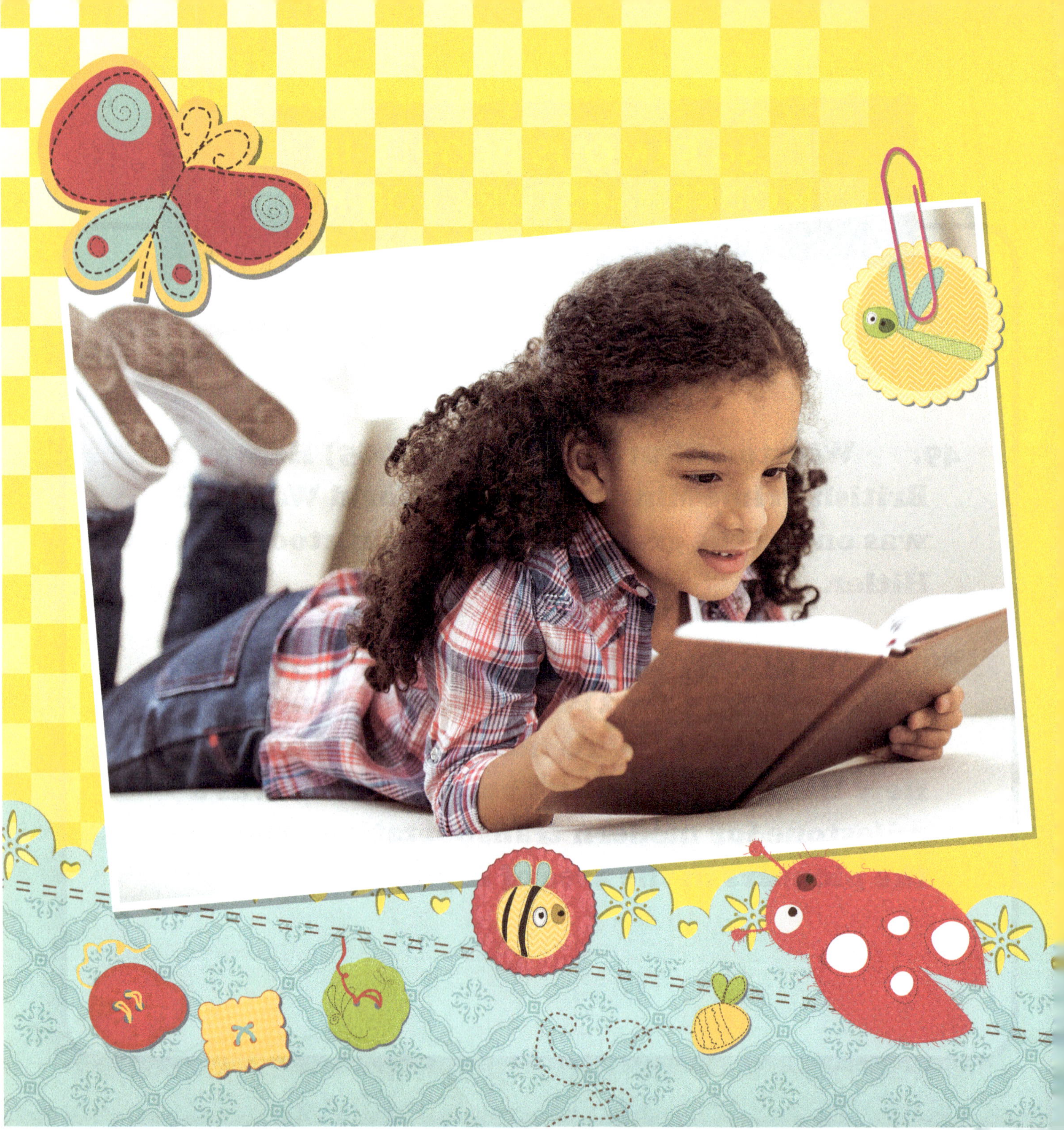

Visit

BABY PROFESSOR
EDUCATION KIDS

www.BabyProfessorBooks.com

to download Free Baby Professor eBooks and view our catalog of new and exciting Children's Books

Lightning Source UK Ltd.
Milton Keynes UK
UKOW07f2210251017
311622UK00006B/89/P